Knit Christmas Ornament

Cute Knit Christmas Tree Ornament Patterns To Make Your Home Beautifully

Copyright © 2020

All rights reserved.

DEDICATION

The author and publisher have provided this e-book to you for your personal use only. You may not make this e-book publicly available in any way. Copyright infringement is against the law. If you believe the copy of this e-book you are reading infringes on the author's copyright, please notify the publisher at: https://us.macmillan.com/piracy

Contents

Christmas Tree 1
Twinkle Twinkle Christmas Star 26
Yarnie Ornament 32
Knitted Snowflakes 36
Mini Christmas Stockings 41
Crochet Snowman Pattern 54
Gingerbread Man Ornament 63

Christmas Tree

Knit Christmas Ornament

I gathered what I had and spent a few minute cruising pinterest for ideas. I saw this picture of a Christmas tree ornament that was basically a dead pin, meaning all I had to guide me was a picture, no instructions.

It took me about an hour to figure out how to make it work, and another hour to make it , and yes I know in 2 hours I could have driven to the store picked out an ornament, driven home, showered and been dressed for the party, instead of the rushing around I ended up doing that evening. However, I really loved the way it turned out and I think a handmade Christmas ornament means so much more than one from a store.

I tweaked the pattern the second time around, and I like it even better than I did the first one.

Knit Christmas Ornament

Knit Christmas Ornament

Here are the materials you need for this Christmas ornament

- size 7 needles (I use bamboo and love them)
- green yarn (I used cotton, but I think other types would do)
- red yarn (again I used cotton, but you can use other types I do however think the type you use should be the same for both colors)
- buttons for ornaments (I used round but you can use any shape)
- star buttons (I got a large package of these at a yard sale one year)
- small amount of green material (I just used an old t-shirt for this)
- ribbon (I used some that I had bought on clearance, basically anything small enough to fit in the hole of the star button, will work)
- Yarn needle (eye has to be big enough for yarn to go through)
- needles for sewing on buttons

Knit Christmas Ornament

Start your christmas tree by casting on 3 stiches

You are going to start by knitting up the tree first. To get it started cast on 3 stitches making sure that you leave an ample enough tail end to do use in the knitting together stage (say 3 or 4 inches).

Knit Christmas Ornament

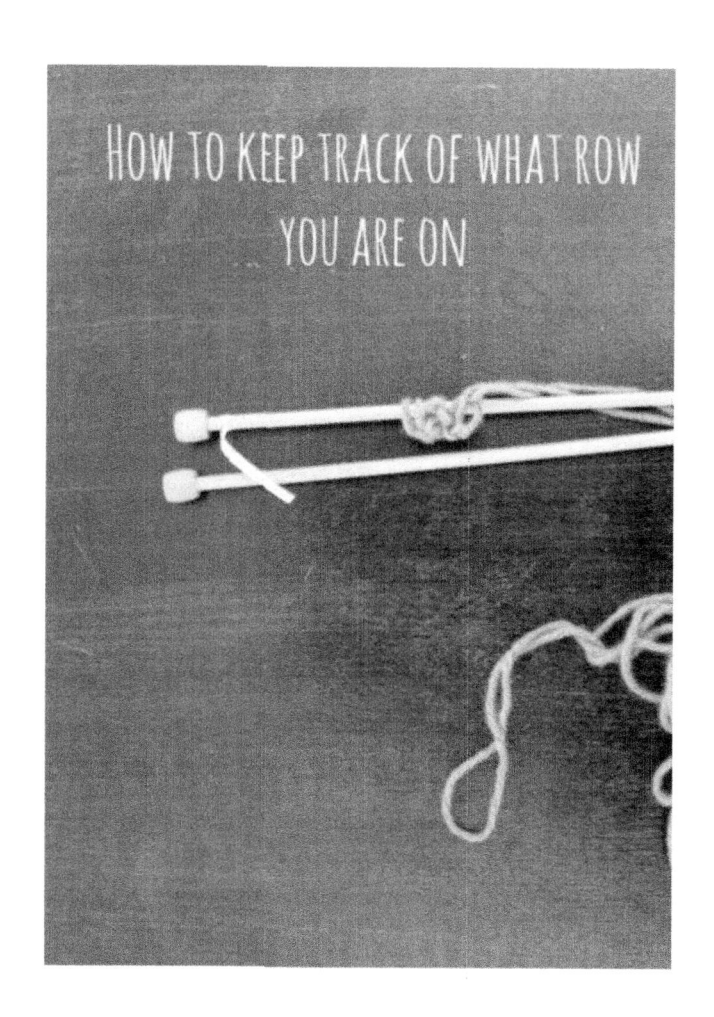

How to keep track of what row you are on

Knit Christmas Ornament

Now comes the tricky part. The pattern has a pattern of increasing that I found a bit hard to remember but I did find a few tricks that made it easier.

The pattern for the Christmas tree sides is as follows

- knit one, knit in front and back in second (like you do a wash cloth, so that you make 2 stitches out of one) then knit to end of row.
- knit full row
- knit until second to last stitch then in that stitch knit in front and back (so that you are again making 2 stitches out of one) then knit last stitch.
- knit full row
- repeat until you have 16 stitches on your needles
- knit a full row
- cast off your row
- At this point one side of your Christmas tree will be complete and then you can repeat the whole process over to make the other side.

Knit Christmas Ornament

To help me remember if I was near the start of a row, or near the end of the row, or if it was a non-increase row I did the following

- I put a twist tie on the end of one needle, which helped me know if this was an increase row or not. Each time I was loading stitches to that needle I knew was an increase row, each time I was unloading stitches I knew it was a non-increase row
- I made a chart on a piece of scrap paper that said F E F E F E F E………..This meant increase in front of row, increase near end of row. I crossed it off each time I did it so I knew what to do next time I was knitting an increase row.
- You could also do a chart that goes like this F N E F N E F N E…….. This would eliminate need for twist tie as the N would stand for the non-increase row.

Once your two Christmas tree pieces are done it is time to work the ends in so that they are hidden.

Essentially all you do is thread the tails on your needle one at a time and then work each one into the stitches itself. I like to work through at least half a dozen or so and then un-thread your needle and cut off the yarn sticking out.

Now it is time to cut your material (um...ya I know the ends are not done in this picture, it is out of sequence but really it doesn't matter what order you do these two steps). The cutting doesn't have to be perfect, as you can see from mine. What matters is that the pieces of material take up most of the inside of each tree but do not spill out the sides.

Also as long as the material is green so that it blends in between the holes of the knitting it doesn't matter what type it is. I used an old t-shirt of my daughter's, since it was free.

Now you want to make a tree sandwich, putting one knitted side on the bottom then the two green pieces of material and then the other knitted tree. Play around with them a bit until you have them all laying flat and all the green material is safely within the knitted sides.

TIME TO SEW UP THE PIECES INTO ONE TREE

To sew the piece together cut off one piece of yarn roughly the length from you finger tips to mid bicep. I tied mine on to one corner of the tree, leaving a long tail to work in just like I did when the tree was in two pieces. Slip stitch around the tree watching your tension not so loose that you have gaps but not so tight that it causes puckering.

Knit Christmas Ornament

WHEN YOUR TREE IS DONE YOU SHOULD END UP WITH A TREE THAT IS AROUND 6 INCHES IN HIEGHT

When my tree was put together is was right around 6 inches in height. Of course yours might be smaller or bigger depending on your tension, so let this be your guide and not a strict rule. After I was done stitching the sides of the tree together I knotted together the ends and then stabbed them into the tree with the yarn needle so that they were hidden.

Knit Christmas Ornament

NOW TO ATTACH THE BUCKET THE CHRISTMAS TREE SITS IN

To attach the red bucket to the Christmas tree you need to work your needle into a few of the bottom stitches. I did this by folding the tree in half and taking 2 on one side and 3 on the other. I suppose you could make it 3 on each side since there really was no plan to my bucket except that it look like it was in the middle and not too small but not too big and 5 stitches looked about right to me.

Knit Christmas Ornament

KNIT 8 ROWS TO MAKE YOU TREE BUCKET

Work the red yarn in the green . Knit 8 rows of it and then cast off. Leave a long red tail at end. I knotted the red yarn to the green yarn near the first stitch after I casted off. I don't know if that is the proper way to do it but it worked.

To finish the bucket I folded the red bucket in half. I knotted the two ends together and then used the long tail of yarn I left to slip stitch the red yarn to the bottom of the green tree and then closed one side. I then used the other tail to slip stitch the other side shut. After the bucket was all sewn shut I cut off all but an inch or so of the yarn tales and then used the needle to hide them in the bucket.

Once you complete the tree you are going to want to decorate it. You can use matching colorful buttons like I did. So that each side of the tree looks the same or you can use random buttons on either side. I had a friend who made some of these trees for her aunt and used buttons from her aunt's antique button collection. It meant a lot to the aunt to see her pretty buttons on display on her tree.

DECIDE HOW YOU WANT TO LAY OUT YOUR BUTTONS BEFORE YOU START SEWING THEM ONE

TIP: SNAP A PICTURE WITH YOUR CELL PHONE SO THAT YOU CAN LOOK AT IT IF NEEDED.

Once you know what buttons you want to decorate your tree, take some time deciding just where you want them. Once you have them arranged in a way you like, snap a picture with your cell phone before removing them all. This will give you something to look at should you forget where you wanted them.

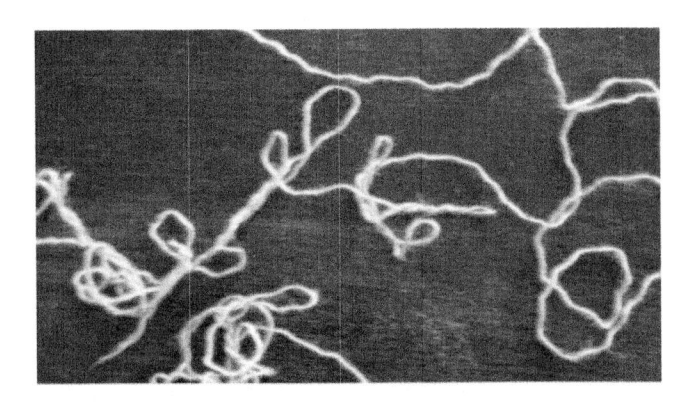

Instead of running out to the store to find matching green thread, I snipped off a piece of yarn and split the four strands up. This way I had an exact match to the yarn . You can use green thread though if you rather. I won't report you to the thrifty police LOL.

Knit Christmas Ornament

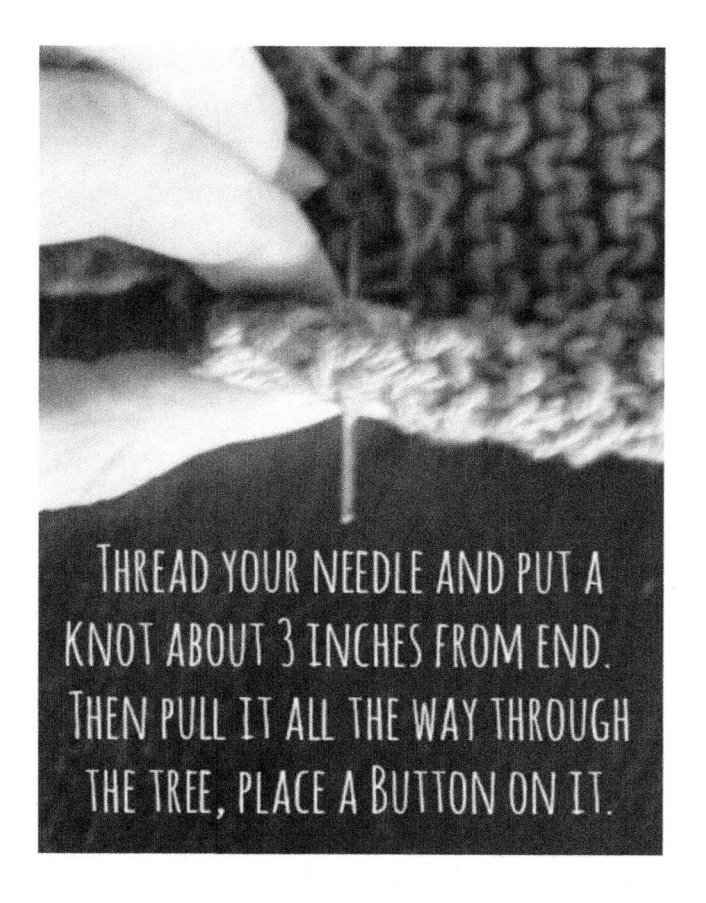

> THREAD YOUR NEEDLE AND PUT A KNOT ABOUT 3 INCHES FROM END. THEN PULL IT ALL THE WAY THROUGH THE TREE, PLACE A BUTTON ON IT.

To put your buttons on securely, first thread your needle and then put a knot about 3 inches away from end. Pull the thread through the entire tree and stop at knot. Place the needle through one button hole and pull it down the thread then insert button into other hole and through the tree again to another button on the other side.

> GO BACK AND FORTH BETWEEN THE TWO BUTTONS 4 OR SO TIMES UNTIL THE BUTTONS ON EITHER SIDE ARE SECURELY FASTENED IN PLACE

Go through from one button to the other 4 or so times until the buttons on either side are securely in place.

Knit Christmas Ornament

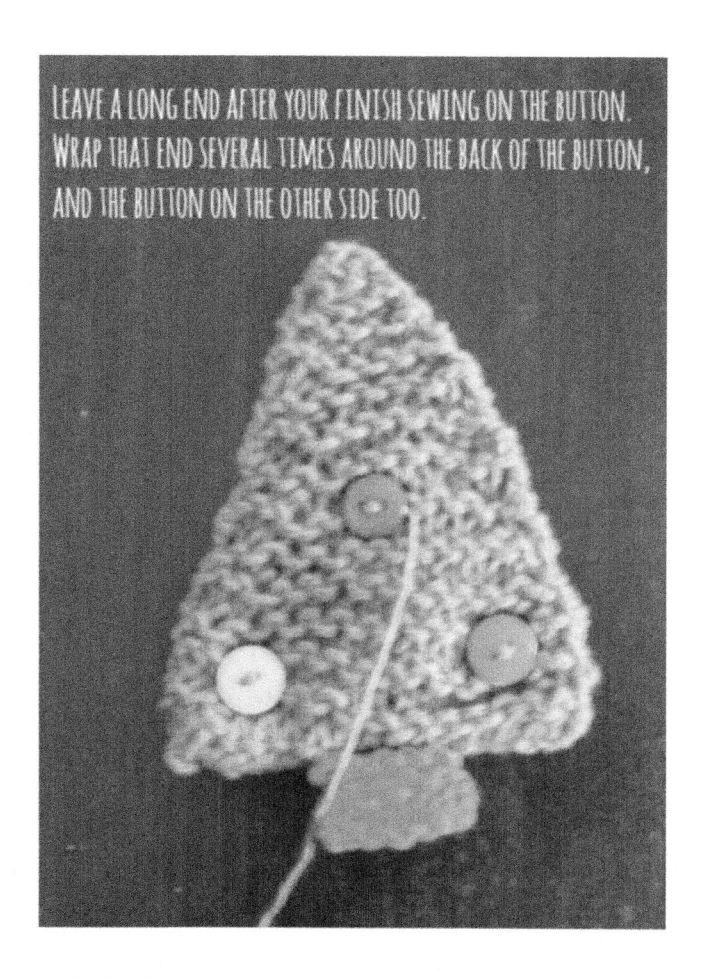

To finish off the buttons once you are done securing them to tree take the ends of the thread on both sides and wrap them around the base of the buttons. This will hide the ends.

Attaching Star To Top Of Knitted Christmas Tree

How you attach the star to the top of the Christmas tree is really going to depend on what type of star button you find. The ones I currently have are more like beads with holes through the middle.

To attach them I first thread them onto a narrow ribbon.

I then used the needle to poke the ribbon through the top of the Christmas tree. and pulled it through the star bead again. To finish it I knotted it just above the star, so that it won't move much, and then knotted the top of the ribbon so that it will hang on the tree.

And with that it was done!

I really like how it turned out and plan to make several more to give as gifts.

Twinkle Twinkle Christmas Star

Continuing with our **Christmas knitting patterns**, today it's time for an adorable little star. Easy, fun and quick to knit, if you like to knit, yule love this pattern!

This is a seven-point star, and you can knit it in one or more colors, there are no rules. Neither is it necessary to follow a specific gauge, use what you have at home (just keep in mind that the thicker the yarn, and the bigger the needles, the larger your star will be).

Besides, the Christmas star is the perfect project for decorating your tree or to give away, while making use of your stash (as well as the **Christmas Tree knitting pattern**).

To form the seven points of the star, we'll be knitting seven elements or parallelograms. As the first one is finished, we bind off and pick up stitches for the following one.

One more thing: Always cast on an odd number of stitches and complete 2 stripes less than the number of stitches you started with. For example: If you cast on 13 stitches, each element will have 9 stripes.

Let's get started!

Abbreviations

st: Stitch

k: Knit

p: Purl

Knit Christmas Ornament

CA: color A (red)

CB: color B (white)

k2tog: Knit two stitches together

kfb: Knit one stitch front and back

yfwd: Yarn forward (bring the yarn in front of the work)

s1: Slip 1 stitch as if to purl

Materials

8 gr of worsted weight wool or n° 4 (or cotton yarn, whatever you have at home). 5 gr red and 3 gr white

2 x 4 mm / US 8 knitting needles

Tapestry needle, scissors

Measurement of the finished star

10 x 10 cm / 4 x 4 in

How to knit a Christmas Star

N.B.:

All the elements have 5 color stripes (always finishing with the same color we started).

Every color stripe includes two rows. The color change happens after knitting two rows in the same color.

The stitch count keeps the same: After knitting every row, before binding off the element, and after picking up the stitches for the next element, we will always have the same number of stitches.

CO an odd number of stitches with CA (for the video demonstration, I cast on 7 st).

Set up rows:

row 0: K across

row 01: Kfb, k to last 2 st, k2tog. This is the first stripe of the star.

Rows that will be repeated from now on:

row 1: With CB, Kfb, k to last 2 st, k2tog.

row 2: P1, K to last st, yfwd, s1. This is the second stripe.

Repeat rows 1 y 2 alternating CA and CB, until 5 stripes are completed. The last stripe is in CA.

To finish the first element, BO knitwise after the 5th stripe, using CA. Keep the last st on the right-hand needle. Cut CB leaving a 2 in / 5 cm tail. The first element or parallelogram has been finished.

With CA, pick up 6 st of the left side of the element. There are 7 st.

Knit Christmas Ornament

*Next row: K across (row 0).

Next row: With CA, repeat rows 1 and 2, alternating CB and CA, until 5 stripes are completed. Close this second element, and pick up 6 st to start the 3º element.

Repeat the process from *, until 7 elements are completed.

Join the first and seventh elements, weave in the ends, and make a hanging loop. And enjoy your Christmas star!

Yarnie Ornament

This knit Christmas ornament is the ultimate gift for any yarn lover. Adorn your tree with your passion for knitting with this Yarnie Ornament. Knit a little knitting basket and wind teeny balls of yarn for a miniature yarn stash that you'll be sure to love. You can even make tiny knitting needles. While knitters know that needles are the way to go, you could even make a little hook and make a gift for the crochet lover in your life. Make several of these

Knit Christmas Ornament

adorable DIY ornament for your own tree or give a few as gifts to the ladies in your knitting club.

Knitting Needle Size9 or 5.5 mm

Yarn Weight(4) Medium Weight/Worsted Weight and Aran (16-20 stitches to 4 inches)

Gauge stitches, rows, inches.

Materials:

- STITCH NATION 1 ball each
- STITCH NATION 1 ball 2205 Little Lamb A
- STITCH NATION 1 ball 2925 Passionfruit B
- STITCH NATION 1 ball 2640 Thyme C
- STITCH NATION 1 ball 2910 Poppy D
- STITCH NATION 1 ball 2510 Aquamarine E
- Knitting Needles: 5.5mm [US 9]
- Yarn needle
- 2 toothpicks
- 2 round beads
- Craft glue

Knit Christmas Ornament

Gauge: Gauge is not critical for this project.

Measurements: Finished basket measures 3½" x 3".

Abbreviations:

- A, B, C = colors A, B, C
- K = knit
- mm = millimeters
- p = purl
- st(s) = stitch (es)
- * or ** = repeat whatever follows the * or ** as indicated

Instructions:

Pattern:

Seed St (Worked over an odd number of sts)

Row 1: K1 * p1, k1; repeat from * across.

Repeat Row 1 for Seed st.

Basket

With A, cast on 19 sts. Marking first row as the right side, work in Seed st until piece measures 2½" from beginning, end by working a wrong side row.

Divide for Handle: Bind off first 8 sts, continue in pattern over next 3 sts (including st on needle after bind-off) for basket handle, bind off remaining 8 sts.

Join yarn to remaining sts and work even until handle measures 4" or desired length for hanging. Bind off.

Finishing

Fold basket in half and sew side seam. Sew end of handle to top edge of basket at seam. Sew bottom seam.

Wind off a small ball (about 1" in diameter) each of B, C, D and E and arrange in basket. Pin or glue ends in place. Glue bead to tip of each toothpick for knitting needles and place in basket as desired.

Knitted Snowflakes

DIY Knitted Snowflakes are an evening or two of easy knitting once you get into the swing of it. I'd like to show you how to knit Sharon's snowflake pattern as the directions had me struggling for awhile until I figured it out.

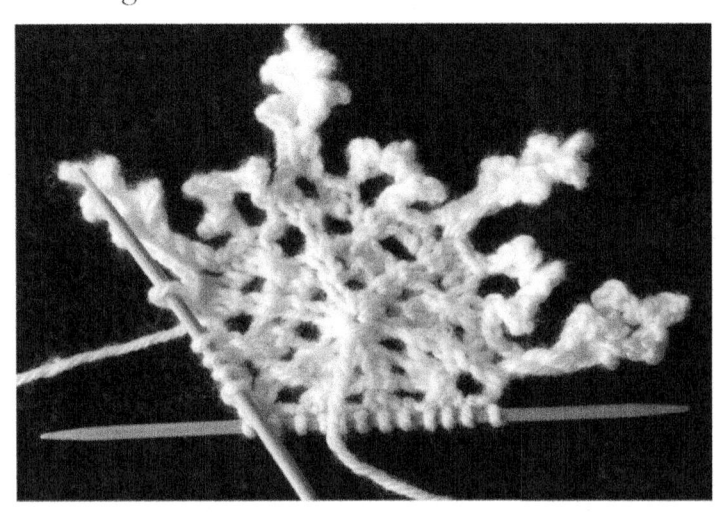

Knit Christmas Ornament

Follow the snowflake pattern and create the circular part of the snowflake on 3 double point needles

Knit Christmas Ornament

The finishing of the snowflake is simple and requires a little spray starch. Simply wet the snowflake, lay it on a towel and spread out the points, pinning each one individually.

Knit Christmas Ornament

The original plan was to hang the snowflakes in the window, but I can see they would look great on the Christmas Tree or hanging in a grouping from the ceiling in the staircase.

Knit Christmas Ornament

Mini Christmas Stockings

41

I knit this stocking flat because I don't enjoy knitting in the round and prefer working fair Isle and intarsia designs this way.

I tend to work it on double pointed needles because during heel shaping you need to switch from working one side to the other. You can knit it on regular needles but slide the work across onto a

Knit Christmas Ornament

second needle at appropriate time. Apart from the stocking top it is worked in stocking stitch (knit on right side and purl on reverse)

Materials:

oddments of yarn. I prefer to knit these on 2.75 mm needles with pure cotton 4ply but the pattern will knit up with whatever you prefer. Note, obviously the larger the needle size and thicker the yarn, the larger the finished stocking. Before you start, decide which colour you are going to knit the heel in and cut a length at least 110cm (44") keep to one side for second heel shaping*.

PATTERN:

Cast on 25 sts, **(27 if knitting one of the stranded designs charted below)

rows 1 - 3: knit

row 4: (right side) begin pattern from charts below (if required) work a total of 14 rows of pattern ending with a wrong side row. **if working in one of the stranded / fairisle designs: on last wrong side row of pattern chart decrease 1 stitch at either end to give 25 stitches

Knit Christmas Ornament

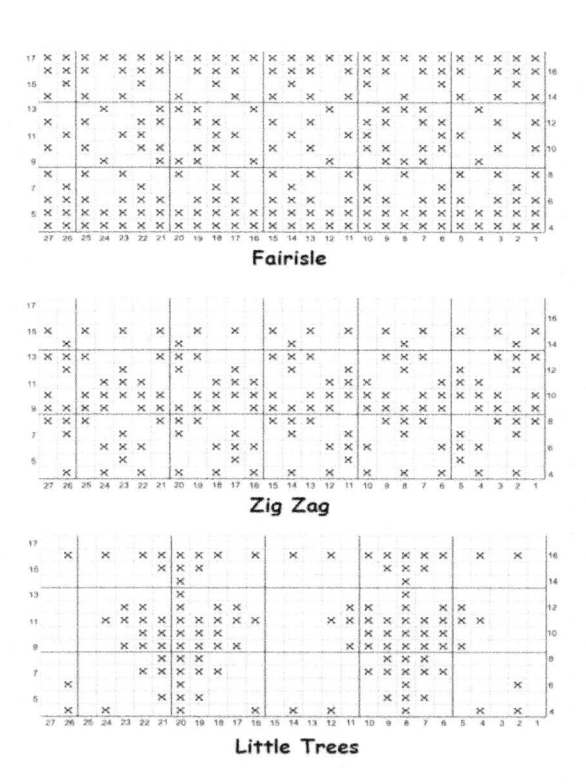

Fairisle

Zig Zag

Little Trees

Start at the bottom of the chart for the pattern charts

<u>Heel shaping</u>:

45

I like to use different coloured yarn to accentuate heel. The heel is worked in 2 halves.

row 18: with right side facing, k7 and turn leaving remaining stitches on needle

row 19: slip 1, p6

repeat these 2 rows 3 more times until 8 rows of heel have been worked

row 26: k3, k2tog through the back, k1, turn leaving 1 remaining stich of heel on needle (see photo step 1)

row 27: slip 1, p4

row 28: k2, k2tog through the back, turn leaving remaining 2 stiches on needle

row 29: slip 1, p2

row 30: k2, k2tog through the back, k1, turn

row 31: slip 1, p3

leaving these 4 stitches on needle with the main part of the stocking, slide all the work along needle, turn with wrong side facing and resume working the other side of the heel (see photo step 2).

reverse row 18: with wrong side facing and using 110cm length of yarn cut earlier*, p7 and turn leaving remaining stitches on needle

reverse row 19: slip 1, k6

repeat these 2 rows 3 more times until 8 rows of heel have been worked

reverse row 26: p3, p2tog, p1, turn leaving 1 remaining stich of heel on needle

reverse row 27: slip 1, k4

reverse row 28: p2, p2tog, turn leaving remaining 2 stiches on needle

reverse row 29: slip 1, k2

reverse row 30: p2, p2tog, p1, turn

reverse row 31: slip 1, k3

row 32: with right side facing rejoin main colour and begin knitting across first 4 stitches of heel shaping, pick up 5 stitches from inside edge of heel (see photo step 3), knit 11 stitches across main part of stocking, pick up 5 stitches from inside edge of 2nd heel half and knit final 4 stitches (29 stitches on needle) (see photo step 4)

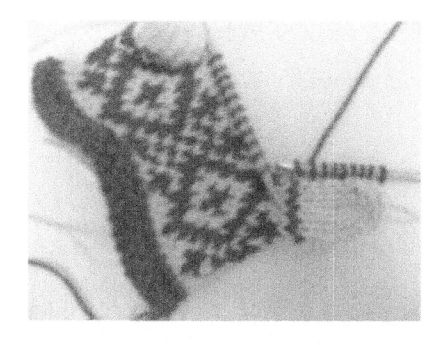

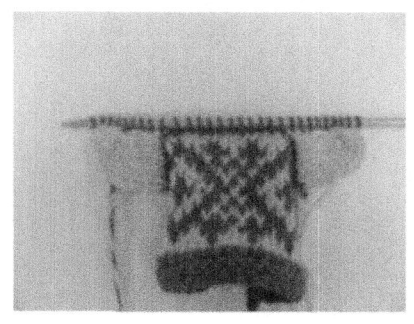

row 33: purl

row 34: K8, k2tog, k9, k2tog through the back, k8

row 35: p7, p2tog through the back, p9, p2tog, p7

row 36: K6, k2tog, k9, k2tog through the back, k6 (23 stitches)

row 37: purl work a further 8 rows of stocking stitch (knit on right side, purl on reverse)

row 46: with right side facing change colour for toe cap (see photo step 5) and work 2 rows

row 48: K3, K2tog through the back, k4, k2tog, k1, k2tog through the back, k4, k2tog, k3

row 49: purl

row 50: K3, K2tog through the back, k2, k2tog, k1, k2tog through the back, k2, k2tog, k3 (15 stitches) (see photo step 6)

row 51: purl

Making Up:

Cut work from the ball leaving a long end for sewing up. Thread end through 15 stitches on needle (see photo step 7) and pull up tight.

Join seam running up bottom and back of stocking using mattress stitch (see photo step 8).

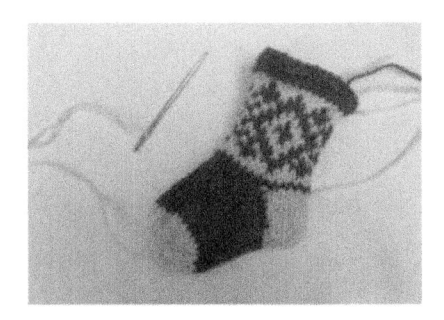

Turn inside out and tie up all ends securely and trim - no need to sew them in. Turn right side out.

Hanging loop: cast on 35 stitches and then cast them off. Double strip over to make a loop and sew to back of stocking. Secure with a cute button.

Knit Christmas Ornament

Knit Christmas Ornament

Crochet Snowman Pattern

Knit Christmas Ornament

Your holiday decorating won't be complete without this cozy crochet snowman amigurumi! I'm envisioning a whole family of them sitting on my mantel ☺ They would also make a wonderful handmade gift for kids and adults!

Materials:

-Worsted weight yarn in white, black, and red. I used Lion Brand Vanna's Choice.

-Size G6 (4mm) Crochet Hook

-Safety Eyes (Black, 6mm)

-Tapestry needle

-Poly-fil stuffing

-Poly-fil beads/ Poly-pellets*

-Stitch marker

*Although you could stuff the entire snowman with regular poly-fil stuffing, I recommend weighting the bottom of it with Poly-Pellets so your snowman will easily stand upright. Poly-Pellets are small plastic beads. You can find them at craft stores like Michaels and Jo-Anns or you can buy them online at Amazon. Do not try to replace poly-fil pellets with rice or beans. They will invite little pests into your crochet and if they get wet they can breakdown and mold. Also, you probably don't want to put your poly-pellets directly inside the crocheted piece. Overtime the yarn could stretch and the pellets could fall out. Not safe for young children. I put my pellets inside an old pair of baby stockings. I just cut the foot off, poured the pellets in (enough to make a nice ball at the bottom of the snowman) and tied it off.

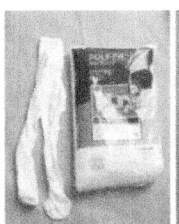

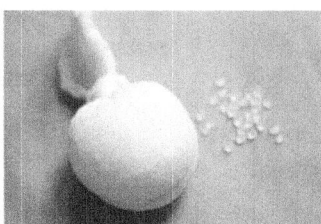

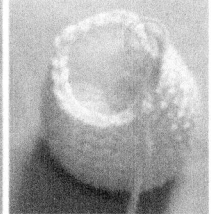

Knit Christmas Ornament

Abbreviations:

<u>Magic Ring Tutorial</u>

SC = Single Crochet

SC Decrease = Single Crochet Decrease

Crochet Snowman Pattern

Finished snowman measure approx. 6" tall (from hat to bottom) and 3" at its widest point.

Magic ring, chain 1 and make 10 SC inside ring, pull tight and continue to SC in rounds (do not join). Use a stitch marker to keep track of your rows if needed.

Rd 2: 2 SC in first stitch, SC in next stitch, repeat around (15 SC)

Rd 3: 2 SC in first stitch, SC in next 2 stitches, repeat around (20 SC)

Rd 4: 2 SC in first stitch, SC in next 3 stitches, repeat around (25 SC)

Knit Christmas Ornament

Rd 5: 2 SC in first stitch, SC in next 4 stitches, repeat around (30 SC)

Rd 6-10: SC in each stitch around (30 SC)

Rd 11: SC Decrease, SC in next 4 stitches, repeat around

Rd 12: SC in each stitch around (25 SC)

Rd 13: SC Decrease, SC in next 3 stitches, repeat around

Fill with your polyfil beads and add button safety eyes

Rd 14: SC Decrease, SC in next 2 stitches, repeat around

Rd 15: 2 SC in first stitch, SC in next 2 stitches, repeat around (20 SC)

Rd 16: 2 SC in first stitch, SC in next 3 stitches, repeat around (25 SC)

Rd 17-19: SC in each stitch around (25 SC)

Rd 20: SC Decrease, SC in next 3 stitches, repeat around

Add eyes and nose

Rd 21: SC Decrease, SC in next 2 stitches, repeat around

Rd 22: SC Decrease, SC in next stitch, repeat around

Stuff with regular polyfil (not beads)

Rd 23: SC Decrease around until closed.

Fasten off and weave in ends.

Carrot Nose:

Chain 4, slip stitch in 2nd chain from hook, slip stitch in next chain, SC in last. Fasten off, sew onto head.

Scarf:
Chain 50, SC in 3rd chain from hook and rest of the way down chain. Fasten off weave in ends. Tie around snowman neck.

Top hat:

Magic ring, chain 1 and make 10 SC in ring, pull tight, join, chain 1

Rd 2: 2 SC in first stitch, SC in next stitch, repeat around, join, chain 1 (15 SC)

Rd 3: in back loops only, SC in each stitch around (15 SC)

Rd 4: now working in both loops, SC Decrease, SC in next 3 stitches, repeat around, join, chain 1

Rd 5-6: SC in each stitch around, join, chain 1 (12 SC)

Rd 7: in front loops only, SC in each stitch around, join, chain 1 (12 SC)

Rd 8: 2 SC in each stitch around, join, fasten off leaving tail to sew on to head.

Add a cute button like a poinsettia. Stuff hat lightly with poly-fil stuffing before sewing onto head.

Let it snow, let it snow, let it snow!

Knit Christmas Ornament

*** You may make and sell products from my patterns but if you do I ask that you link back to my post. Please do not copy and post this pattern and claim it as your own. Please do not re-publish photos as your own.***

Gingerbread Man Ornament

MATERIALS:

- Yarn: Worsted weight cotton yarn (I used Dapper Dreamer Combed Cotton yarn in gingerbread color.

- Hook: 4.0mm crochet hook / US G/5 / UK 8

- Small size white buttons for the eyes and any other color of your choice for decorating the body.

- White zigzag ric rac lace ribbon for the arms and legs

decoration.

ABBREVIATION/STITCHES:

- Magic ring

- sc – single crochet (US) / dc – double crochet (UK)

- st(s) – stitch(es)

- sl st – sip stitch

- inc – increase = two single crochet stitches in the same stitch

- dec – decrease = crochet two stitches together using the invisible decrease method

- [sc, inc] n times – repeat the pattern between parentheses n times.

- (N sts) – number of stitches in a round after finishing round

NOTES:

– **Finished gingerbread man ornament measures approximately 6 inches. Any variations to hook size and**

yarn weight will result in a different sized piece.
– Every separate piece will be worked in continuous rounds, do not join rounds with a slip stitch or chains unless otherwise stated.

– Mark the first stitch of each round by using a stitch marker or a piece of yarn.

PATTERN

ARMS (make 2):

Begin with a magic ring.

Round 1: sc 6

Round 2: inc 6 times (12 sts)

Round 3: sc around

Round 4: sc around

Round 5: sc around

Round 6: sc around

Round 7: sc around

Fasten off and leave a short yarn tail. Set both piece aside for now.

LEGS (make 2):

Begin with a magic ring.

Round 1: sc 6

Round 2: inc 6 times (12 sts)

Round 3: sc around

Round 4: sc around

Round 5: sc around

Round 6: sc around

Round 7: sc around

Fasten off and leave a short yarn tail. Repeat the same steps to make the second leg but do not fasten off, do not cut yarn.

BODY:

Round 1: Join legs with a single crochet in the first stitch of Round 7 of the first leg. Place your stitch marker in the single crochet stitch you just made (counted as your first stitch for the body), sc in each of the remaining 11 sts of first leg and in the next 12 sts of second leg (24 sts)

Knit Christmas Ornament

Round 2: sc around

Round 3: sc around

Round 4: sc 5, dec, sc 10, dec, sc 5 (22 sts)

Round 5: sc around

Round 6: sc 4, dec, sc 10, dec, sc 4 (20 sts)

Round 7: sc around

Round 8: sc 4, dec, sc 8, dec, sc 4 (18 sts)

Round 9: sc around

Round 10: sc 4, dec, sc 7, dec, sc 3 (16 sts)

Round 11: sc 3, dec, sc 7, dec, sc 2 (14 sts)

Round 12: sc 3, dec, sc 5, dec, sc 2 (12 sts)

Do not fasten off, proceed to next steps to crochet the head.

HEAD:

Round 1: [sc, inc] 6x (18 sts)

Round 2: [sc 2, inc] 6x (24 sts)

At this point, sew each arm at the side between Round 7 to Round 12 of the body using whip stitch method (total of 12 whip sts from front to back of each arm).

Now is also the best time to sew the 3 buttons onto the center of the body. This way, you will be able to hide the stitches inside the work. Once done, continue to next Rounds.

Knit Christmas Ornament

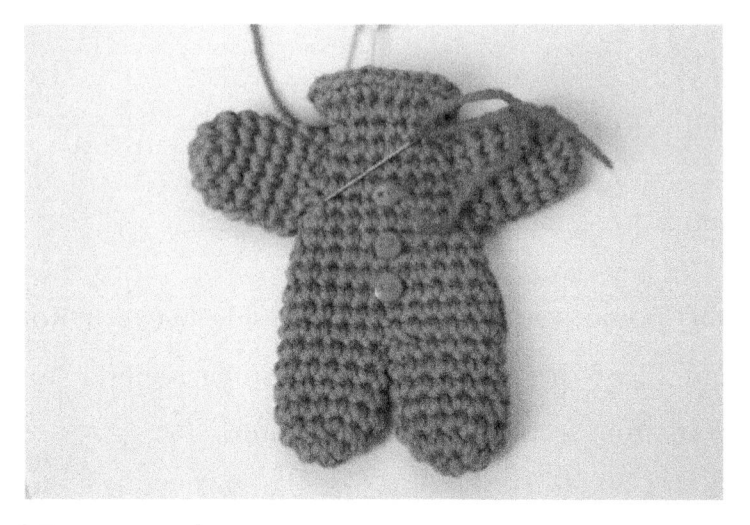

Round 3: sc around

Round 4: sc around

Round 5: sc around

Round 6: [sc 2, dec] 6 times (18 sts)

Round 7: sc around

Sew the white buttons at this point between Round 5 and Round 6 of head. Once done continue to next steps to complete the head.

Round 8: [sc, dec] 6 times (12 sts)

Round 9: dec 6 times

Cut yarn leaving a long tail. If you prefer to crochet the string that you can use to hang the ornament, make sure to leave atleast 2.5 feet long yarn tail. Fasten off then weave through the stitches of last round. Pull tail end gently to close the gap. Crochet 20 chains or more then slip stitch in the any stitch of previous round. Fasten off and hide tail.

Lastly, cut out some zigzag ric rac lace ribbon then place on both arms and legs as shown on photos using fabric glue.

Knit Christmas Ornament

Printed in Great Britain
by Amazon